BOOST
SELF-ESTEEM

Honor Head

W

FRANKLIN WATTS
LONDON • SYDNEY

Published in paperback in Great Britain in 2020
by The Watts Publishing Group
© The Watts Publishing Group 2020

Managing editor: Victoria Brooker
Design: Sophie Burdess

Image Credits: Shutterstock – all images Good Studio
apart from Iveta Angelova & Ollikeballoon
graphic elements throughout;
LOLE 20l, ONYX 21 tc, Zarian 7c.

ISBN: 978 1 4451 7060 2 (hbk)
ISBN: 978 1 4451 7061 9 (pbk)

Printed in China

FSC
www.fsc.org
MIX
Paper from
responsible sources
FSC® C104740

Franklin Watts
An imprint of
Hachette Children's Group
Part of the Watts Publishing Group
Carmelite House
50 Victoria Embankment
London EC4Y 0DZ
An Hachette UK Company
www.hachette.co.uk
www.franklinwatts.co.uk

CONTENTS

WHAT IS SELF-ESTEEM?

Self-esteem is what you think about yourself
and how much you like who you are.

Good or high self-esteem...

That looks scary but I'll give it a try.

I can score this!

I failed last time, but I will pass this time.

I worked so hard for this. I am proud of myself!

I know everyone has new trainers, but I like my old ones.

Wow, my hair looks great today!

4

Bad or low self-esteem ...

You can change your self-esteem
and the way you think about yourself.
Just by opening this book you've made a start!

Well done!

1. BELIEVE YOU ARE SPECIAL

Believing you are special is not about thinking you should have all the attention and everyone running around after you. It is about accepting that you are you, faults and all, and believing that you deserve to be successful and happy.

LEARN FROM YOUR MISTAKES AND MOVE ON

LOOK FORWARD TO TRYING AGAIN

JOIN IN THE CONVERSATION – YOU HAVE SOMETHING VALUABLE TO SAY

LIKE WHO YOU ARE

Be proud of how you look, how you think, what you wear and who your friends are. Be yourself.

Set your own goals. These can be short-term goals...

SWIM A LENGTH OF THE POOL

STUDY FOR MY MATHS EXAM

LEARN THAT NEW DANCE

LEARN TO KNIT

FINISH MY BOOK

GO FOR A WALK EVERY DAY

... or goals for the future.

HEART SURGEON

OLYMPIC ATHLETE

BEST-SELLING AUTHOR

BUSINESS OWNER

GAMES DEVELOPER

STAR VLOGGER

DREAM YOUR OWN DREAM

BE AWESOME!

BE BOLD!

GO FOR IT, AS LONG AS IT IS WHAT YOU TRULY WANT!

DO WHAT YOU LOVE

2. BE BODY POSITIVE

What do you see when you look in the mirror?

Poor body image is caused by lots of things, especially film stars and vloggers who look glamorous all the time. They make 'perfection' seem like the ideal and that can make others feel inferior. But underneath the make-up and the clothes, they're the same as all of us.

Remember, whatever you look like, everyone has something special about them to feel proud about.

Self-image is not just about how you look on the outside, it's about who you are inside...

3. GET HEALTHY

A healthy lifestyle helps to keep us physically and mentally fit.
Your body is amazing. It is strong and powerful. Be proud of your body.

Exercise not only keeps you fit, it makes you feel good.
When you do exercises that make your heart beat faster,
your body releases chemicals that make you feel happy.
Even washing the car, going for a walk or tidying your room
(yes, really) can give you a sense of having achieved something.

MAKE YOUR HEART PUMP FASTER TO STAY FIT

STRETCH OUT TO BUILD STRENGTH AND STAY SUPPLE

Worried about your weight? See a doctor who can give you advice about how to get healthy.

Did you know that food can affect our emotions and thinking?
Too much fast food, ready-made meals, sugar and fried food
can make us tired, grumpy, thick-headed and feel down
about ourselves and the world.

Eat great, think great

Feel sluggish, think sluggish

Super sleep

After all that good food and exercise
you will probably sleep better, too. Getting
a good night's sleep can make you feel
more positive about yourself.

4. CHANGE YOUR THINKING

A quick switch in how you think can boost your self-esteem.
These examples show easy ways you can change the way you think.

That was a great test paper, well done, but question D was not quite right.

I am so useless at science.

WHAT'S WRONG WITH MARY'S THINKING?

She is filtering out the good things her teacher said and only hearing the negative comments.

QUICK SWITCH:

I'm pleased I did well. I'll do some research into question D for next time.

Ahmed hasn't rung me back, I must have done something wrong.

WHAT'S WRONG WITH FRED'S THINKING?

People with low self-esteem always think everything is their fault even though there is no reason to think this.

QUICK SWITCH:

I hope Ahmed is okay. I haven't heard from him. I'll go round and see him.

Instead of talking down your achievements, be proud of them, no matter how small they are.

I only got top marks because the questions were so easy.

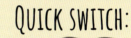

QUICK SWITCH:

Great, top marks! All that revision paid off.

No point in asking to join in, they won't want me.

Is the boy a mind reader? I don't think so! Because of low self-esteem he is assuming the others won't want to let him join them.

QUICK SWITCH:

That looks fun. I'll see if they want an extra player.

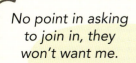

I am so useless at this. I'll never play again.

People with high self-esteem realise that they need to practise to get better instead of thinking they are no good at something.

QUICK SWITCH:

Hmm, looks like I need a bit more practice before the next time!

5. BE POSITIVE

Positive words and thoughts can help you behave in a more positive way. Take time to look in the mirror and say positive things to yourself. These are called affirmations.

I AM KIND AND CARING.

I WILL GET BETTER AT THIS.

I AM PROUD OF ME.

I AM CREATIVE.

I AM FUN TO BE WITH.

I HELP PEOPLE.

I WILL ACHIEVE ANYTHING I WANT.

I CAN DO THIS.

I CAN SUCCEED.

I AM AN IMPORTANT TEAM MEMBER.

I AM STRONG.

I AM A GREAT PERSON TO HAVE AS A FRIEND.

I WILL TRY NEW THINGS.

I LOVE BEING ME.

6. CHANGE YOUR BEHAVIOUR

Part of improving our self-esteem is to behave in a positive way. Try and turn negative behaviour into positive behaviour. It may be hard at first, but it will get easier.

My friend really upset me, but I don't want to make a fuss.

You really upset me. Can we talk about it?

Any decision I make is bound to be wrong.

I've decided what I want to do.

No point in bothering to revise. I'm going to fail anyway.

I'm going to do my best in the exams, so I'd better get revising.

Strong, positive body language will help you to behave in a more positive way.

Make eye contact. This shows you are interested and confident.

Sit and stand up straight. Good posture will help your breathing and make you feel more confident.

Smile at people! It will make you feel better as well.

Take deep breaths before you enter a room or start a conversation, to calm your mind.

Don't fidget, tap your fingers or feet, shuffle or look around all the time. Try and keep your hands, feet and body relaxed.

7. BE ASSERTIVE

Being assertive is not the same as being aggressive, rude, nasty or demanding.

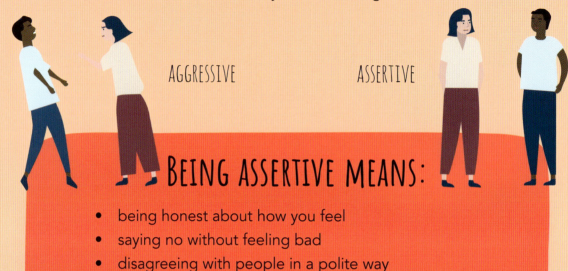

AGGRESSIVE

ASSERTIVE

BEING ASSERTIVE MEANS:

- being honest about how you feel
- saying no without feeling bad
- disagreeing with people in a polite way
- calmly asking for what you want or need
- expressing your own opinions and thoughts.

DON'T BE PASSIVE

If you feel that you always have to please others and ignore your own feelings and wishes, you could end up...

FRUSTRATED

ANGRY

RESENTFUL

HATING YOURSELF

Think before you speak

I would love to go for a walk.

It doesn't matter what I want to do.

I really like the blue one.

I don't care which colour I have.

I really don't have an opinion.

I thought it was a great film.

Practise 'I' and 'My'

I feel...

I'd like...

My favourite is...

I'd prefer...

My choice is...

Your wishes and opinions matter as much as anyone else's.

8. BE CONFIDENT

Being confident is about how you feel about yourself and your abilities. Increasing self-confidence builds up self-esteem.

Ways to boost self-confidence...

Learning something new helps to boost self-esteem.
If you try something and it doesn't work, it may not be for you.
Have a go at something else, but never stop trying!

Don't compare yourself to others

We all have different skills and abilities, likes and dislikes.
Don't be embarrassed to be yourself.

When you feel afraid of trying something new,
channel that fear into energy to help you do your best.
Be your own superhero!

9. DON'T FEAR FAILURE

Low self-esteem can often lead to a fear of failure.
This causes problems such as:

ANXIETY

FEELING SICK

FEAR

SLEEPLESS NIGHTS

STRESS

NOT EATING

PANIC

I'm finishing my revision for the exam tonight.

I'm not going to bother. I know I'll fail.

If I don't get top marks, it will be a disaster.

I was going to try that new sport's club, but I'll do it another time.

WHICH PERSON HERE HAS FEAR OF FAILURE?

WAIT! FAILING IS GOOD FOR YOU!

Really?

Failing and trying again builds up your confidence.

Failing makes you realise people love you and want to be with you for who you are, not what you've achieved.

When you fail, you try again and get better and better.

Failing gives you courage to try new things.

Break out of your comfort zone!

Our comfort zone is the space where we feel comfortable with people and situations we know. Breaking free of your comfort zone means you have more fun, are more interesting and won't get bored!

COMFORT ZONE

Be brave, take a risk.
that is what makes life exciting!

10. CONTROL YOUR SOCIAL MEDIA

Social media use can cause low self-esteem.
But how?

Others seem to be having a better time, making us feel boring and dull

Glamorous people making us feel that we are not good enough

FOMO (fear of missing out) is thinking that if we are not available all the time we will lose friends and miss out

Making us feel worthless if we don't get enough likes

Cyberbullying making us feel scared and alone

THESE ARE ALL POSSIBLE SCREEN-DEMONS THAT CAN MAKE US FEEL LOW.

IF YOUR SOCIAL MEDIA LIFE MAKES YOU FEEL LIKE ANY OF THESE THEN...

... STOP! Take Control!

Enjoy the life you have.

Spend face-to-face time with friends and family.

Try new hobbies and clubs.

Have digital-free times – it can be an hour twice a day, then try a whole day and what about a whole week?

Focus on the positive, being strong and healthy, having a supportive family and good friends.

Block bullies and report cyberbullying to a trusted adult, your school or the police.

Look for vloggers who make you feel good about yourself or have a shared interest.

SHOW THE SCREEN WHO'S IN CHARGE!

11. BUILD UP YOUR LIFE SKILLS

Building life skills will develop strong self-esteem.
Relationship skills help you to build supportive friendships.

Accept not everyone will want to be your friend.

Don't judge other people.

Be a good listener.

Realise other people are scared or nervous, too.

Learn to laugh at yourself.

Be kind and honest.

Accept not everyone will agree with you.

Don't be nasty to others, online or face-to-face.

Accept others' mistakes as well as your own.

Be loyal.

Coping skills will help you when life gets tough.

Feeling anxious about something? Visualise it going well. Take a few minutes to close your eyes and see yourself succeeding. Believe you can do it. Then take a deep breath and go!

Feeling stressed? Find somewhere quiet, close your eyes, slowly breathe in through your nose and out through your mouth until you feel calmer.

Learn to talk to someone when things get tough – a friend, family member, online forum or helpline.

Write down your worries and fears... they can look less scary on paper.

12. BE KIND TO YOURSELF

Always putting yourself down? Take some time out to think about how wonderful you really are.

WRITE DOWN 5 THINGS...

- ✓ … you really like about yourself

- ✓ … you like about your appearance

- ✓ … that make you feel happy

- ✓ … you would like to achieve in the next year

- ✓ … that make you proud of yourself

THAT'S LOADS OF THINGS THAT ARE REALLY COOL ABOUT YOU!

MY BOOK OF ME

Write out a list of the things you are good at and anything that makes you happy. Look at this when you feel you can't do anything right. Add something new to your book every day.

I make people laugh.

I make the best cheese sandwiches.

I can tap dance.

My cat loves me!

I love my cat!

I am great at spelling.

I am learning to cook.

I am patient.

I love listening to music.

I visit granny every week.

I am loyal to my friends.

I always help with the housework.

I work hard at school.

I scored the best goal of the season.

I AM SPECIAL ... I AM ME!

WHERE TO GET HELP

Talk to your carers, a trusted adult, a teacher or your friends
about how you feel. If there is no one you want to talk to,
there are loads of places online that can help you.

Chat rooms and forums are great for talking to people who
feel the same way as you do and may have had similar experiences.
However never share personal details with anyone, no matter
how genuine they seem. And never meet up with strangers.
Telephone helplines are places where you can talk to someone
who is specially trained to understand what you are going through.
They won't judge you or make you do anything you don't want to do.
You don't have to be embarassed or ashamed or silly
about what you tell them. They will be understanding, kind and supportive.

www.childline.org.uk/info-advice/your-feelings/mental-health
Message or call the 24 hour helpline
for advice or someone who'll just listen.
The helpline is 0800 1111

https://papyrus-uk.org
A place to go if you have thoughts
about harming yourself or suicide.
HopelineUK 0800 068 41 41

www.samaritans.org
A place where anyone can go
for advice and comfort.
The helpline is 08457 90 90 90

www.sane.org/get-help
Help and support for anyone affected
by mental and emotional issues.
The helpline is 0300 304 7000

www.gosh.nhs.uk/children/general-health-advice/eat-smart
How to eat for a better, healthier diet.

https://kidshealth.org/en/kids/self-esteem.html
Tips on how to build your self-esteem.

www.supportline.org.uk
A charity giving emotional support to young people.
The helpline is 01708 765200

kidshealth.org/en/kids/feeling
Advice on managing emotions.

www.youngminds.org.uk
Advice for young people
experiencing bullying, stress
and mental or emotional anxieties.

www.brainline.org/article/who-me-self-esteem-people-disabilities
How to boost self-esteem regardless of disabilities.

SHOUT!
A text-only 24/7 helpline for anyone suffering from
emotional and mental issues or going through a crisis.
Text 85258 and a trained volunteer will be there to help.

Or settle down with a book...

**You Are Awesome: Find Your Confidence
and Dare to be Brilliant at (Almost) Anything**
by Matthew Syed, Wren & Rook 2018

**Your Mind Matters: Self-Esteem
and Confidence**
by Honor Head, Franklin Watts, 2017

GLOSSARY

anxiety a feeling of being worried and nervous

assertive being able to express your own opinions and wants in a way
  that is not aggressive

confident believing that you can do something

filtering removing something that is not wanted

inferior not as good

negative bad; negative feelings make you feel sad and miserable and not good enough

passive letting things happen even if you don't want them to

positive good; positive feelings make you feel strong and confident

posture the way you hold your body when you move

resentful angry or bitter

self-image how you see yourself

sluggish feeling slow and tired

visualise to see yourself doing something you want to achieve in your mind

INDEX